# Clay Pots and Bones

# Pka'wo'qq aq Waqntal

## Lindsay Marshall

# Clay Pots and Bones

# Pka'wo'qq aq Waqntal

## Lindsay Marshall

## New Edition

Cape Breton University Press
Sydney, Nova Scotia

Cape Breton University Press recognizes the support of the Province of Nova Scotia, through Film and Creative Industries Nova Scotia, and the support received for its publishing  program from the Canada Council for the Arts Block Grants Program. We are pleased to work in partnership with these bodies to develop and promote our cultural resources.

FILM & CREATIVE INDUSTRIES
NOVA SCOTIA

Canada Council    Conseil des Arts
for the Arts      du Canada

Cover design: Cathy MacLean, Chéticamp, NS.
Cover image: Mi'kmaw hand crafted basket (19th century). Courtesy Mi'kmaq Resource Centre #2012-15-3979, Cape Breton University.
Layout: Laura Bast, Sydney, NS.
First printed in Canada

Marshall, Lindsay, 1960-, author
    Clay pots and bones : poems / Lindsay Marshall.

Issued in print and electronic formats.
ISBN 978-1-927492-81-9 (pbk.).--ISBN 978-1-927492-82-6 (pdf).--ISBN 978-1-927492-83-3 (epub).--ISBN 978-1-927492-84-0 (mobi)

    I. Title.

PS8576.A7573C52 2014      C811'.54C2014-900530-X
                     C2014-900531-8
Cape Breton University Press
PO Box 5300, 1250 Grand Lake Road
Sydney, NS B1P 6L2 CA
www.cbu.ca/press

## To My Father and Brothers

When this book was first published in February 1997, I dedicated it to my father, Thomas Alexander Marshall.

On April 19, 1997, my father passed away, leaving a gap in the lives of his family and all those who knew him.

Two thousand and thirteen has been a very difficult year for me and my family. We lost Gary Thomas Marshall and Stephen Joseph Marshall in February and October respectively.

I dedicate this edition of *Clay Pots and Bones* to the memory of Tommy Marshall, Gary Thomas Marshall and Stephen Joseph Marshall, a memory that will remain forever strong.

The passage below is an excerpt from a poem entitled "Sealing Secrets from All," which I wrote for my father on his death:

and with a deep breath
that seemed to last forever,
like a wind
arriving on cue with a blessing
he spoke:
"Good Creator,
I am ready."
The still man lay
surrounded by satin,
a single rose
and a tobacco leaf
sealing secrets from all.

# Contents

## Foreword to the First Edition

The expression of one's culture can take many forms. Lindsay Marshall, in this his first book, has chosen to interpret our Mi'kmaw way of life through his poetry.

Lindsay's message is sometimes clear, as in the poem "Now It's Your Turn," but oftentimes the message is more cryptic, as in "Save the Last Bullet."

Although much of the poetry in *Clay Pots and Bones* is very personal, Lindsay manages to express himself in such a way that even the personal has a universal appeal. For instance the poem "To David," which Lindsay wrote for his son, could apply to my own son or daughter. Likewise, the experiences of Donald Marshall Jr. as related in the moving poem "They Took Your Word," can be related to the pain and plight of many.

Lindsay sets out to interpret both the past and the present Mi'kmaw way of life, and although true understanding cannot come from one small book of poetry, Lindsay succeeds in defining the essence of his own being, which I believe is the true hallmark of a true poet.

Dr. Peter Christmas, 1997
*Former Executive Director*
*Mi'kmaq Association for Cultural Studies*

## Acknowledgements

I would like to thank all my brothers and sisters for their continued support and love; my son David for never failing to be at my side when times have been difficult; a woman with whom I first fell in love in grade 7, whose love sustains me and breathes life into my life. We see the world with new eyes and a brand new perspective. My friend, my partner; my Florie Sutherland.

## Petroglyphs

The illustrations contained in this book are copies of rock engravings made many years ago by the Mi'kmaq at Lake Kejimkujik in Nova Scotia. These rock drawings are called petroglyphs. They provide for us a graphic glimpse of the customs, beliefs and everyday activities of the traditional Mi'kmaw way of life. They are not intended here to illustrate Lindsay Marshall's poetry but merely to add another dimension to the poet's own interpretation of his Mi'kmaw heritage.

# Gentle Warrior Woman

*for Dr. Rita Joe*

Sleep my gentle woman
Let all know you've won your battles
Using wisdom, spoken words and your gentle soul
You've moved me, taught me and given me
A love of words.
Step into your birch canoe
And push away from shore.
See the whirls as your paddle moves you
across land and water.
The sun in its orange and clear sky
Grows larger as you point your kwitn
Towards our Grandfather the sun.
When you reach the farthest shore
Remember us, speak of us
And pray for us
Gentle Warrior Woman

## Hello and Welcome

We say in the Spirit of Mandela
At a sacred place where the tools
Of war remain buried
Stand the descendents
Of Henri Membertou.
For as long as the
Rivers flow free,
The winds caress the
Sea bound coast
Mi'kmaq have honoured
The Treaties with Monarchs;
Their successors and subjects.
In the Spirit of Jean Baptiste Cope
We open our arms like Eagle's wings
We raise our voices as songbirds
We walk with pride and purpose
On the grounds of Peace and Friendship
In the land of Mi'kmaq
We say, Kwe' aq Pjila'si

*Translation courtesy of Bernie Francis*

# Kwe' aq Pjila'si

Teli-wtunkatmek wijey aq Wjijaqmijl Mandela
Sape'wik maqmikew ta'n pukmaqnn
Matntimkewe'l me'j etl-utqutasikl
Kaqmultiek wetapeksultiek
Anli Maupltuo'q.
Teli-pkijitk sipu'l,
Wju'snn munsa'matk qasqi-kjikm
Mi'kmaq kepmite'tmi'titl
Ankumkamkewe'l wejiaql Eleke'wa'ki;
Napune'kwi'tiji aq wunaqapemua.
Wjijaqmijk wejiaq Sa'n-Patist Kopo'q
Wnaqa'tunen npitnokominal staqe kitpu wnisqi'
Wenaqintu'tiek staqe sisipaq
Kepmleketaiek aq kjitmiw
Wjit wantaqo'ti aq witaptimkewey
Ula maqmikek Mi'kma'ki
Aq telua'tiek "Kwe'" aq "Pjila'si"

Demasduit, why did you die
sad and alone?
Did they prod, test and
measure your spirit?
Did you see your family
hide and flee?

*Irony Invades the Few*

## Irony Invades the Few

Who were they
peering through the fog
from clandestine
locations among rocks,
sand and shale?
English sport of hounds and
horses, the blood-sport of the
transplants, who found game
in this new lost land.
Eastern rain cries their name,
lunar solstice tides wash
the Royal sins away.
Demasduit, why did you die
sad and alone?
Did they prod, test and
measure your spirit?
Did you see your family
hide and flee?
Does a voice lose its purpose,
or eyes the prophetic view?
The tribal curse lives on in
the eyes of descendants.
How they suffer and weep
for what is forever lost.
Irony invades the few
while their numbers decline
and flee the hunters of
misery.

## Visitors

A white cloud appears on the blue horizon off the shore of
  Unama'ki.
Strangers are coming in strange vessels.
The vessels come nearer and stop.
A splash is heard as the strangers
throw something from the front of the ship,
looks like a tree trunk with a long gnarly root.
The strangers speak in a foreign tongue.
Their skin is pale as the ghosts that haunt our camps at night.
Faces hairy like dogs, yet they stand upright like us, the
  People of the Dawn,
the first people to greet and get blessings
from the sun
as it rises each morn to bless the rest
who live to the west.
How the strangers cower on the shore.
Surely they must think there is no one here.
Come my brothers, let's go away and tonight
we will return.

They have not ventured inland or moved
from the shore since morn.
Perhaps they have heard the spirits
who guard our sleep, protecting us.
It is time we made them welcome.
Let's build a great fire that overlooks
their camp.

It is a good fire, the flames are the first
to dance.
See how high they jump and kick.
Now the drumming starts,
how we dance and sing.
But wait, something is wrong.
They're leaving.
Wait! We welcome you.
Stop! We mean no harm.

They leave. We wonder if
they'll be back.

They have left strange markings
on a piece of wood.

If this man, now a child, could
answer, I would ask him,
"Matchee, where did you
get those brown shoelaces?"

*Brown Shoelaces*

## Brown Shoelaces

Standing at attention Master Corporal Matchee
doesn't smile or say much anymore.
Didn't he know that he, a Red man,
in their Aryan eyes is the low man?
We saw him meticulously polish and
assemble his FNC-1 through an
unblinking eye on foreign soil while
we saw his comrades regurgitate
words and bravado against their
unknowing, unwilling charges.
Long before the pin hit the casing
the finger was working its way
down his back.
Where did Matchee get those
brown shoelaces for his
black combat boots?
Wasn't he under guard?
If this man, now a child, could
answer, I would ask him,
"Matchee, where did you
get those brown shoelaces?
Did someone help you onto a chair
so your new laces could make
you airborne forever?"
A final jump.
Silence from Master Corporal Matchee,
a temporary reprieve for those
higher up the totem with maroon
hats and hands that don't come clean.

## Alexander Standing in Tall Grass
## on Chapel Island

Every summer since his youth
he would make his way across by boat.
A red apparition in blue water.
Carrying his lunch in one hand,
a scythe in the other, he would
walk like a man with a mission.
His purpose to cut the tall grass
for the many who would arrive
to their Mecca.
A resting figure standing alone
on the lonely isle,
leaning with his elbow on the scythe,
chin in hand.
The scent of newly cut hay everywhere,
the light breeze carrying it away.
A bead of sweat running down his face
past the turquoise blue eyes,
the Indian nose, through the white
stubble and falling finally, quickly
evaporating to the air before
hitting the ground.
The once proud tall grass would fall
easily from the steady measured
swings of his scythe,
the slain grass resurrected to
serve as bedding for the
wi'kuoml.
Bunches and bundles to serve as
fire starters for tea and
fourcents.
Nothing will be wasted this day.

## Forth and Back...

After all these years
Leonard, Leonard.
He walks with state-issued shoes
doing Mandela-like paces
back and forth,
forth and back.
Vertical bars dissect his form,
seen only by the population.
Brown eyes peer through iron.
Air moves freely across his
leather-bound hair, his breath
escapes through nooks and crannies,
while his lungs remain rooted,
and not really suited to be inside,
a permanent guest.
Lesser men would have
worn their last necktie or
stood with one shoelace
still tied to the state-issued
shoe while the other...
elsewhere.
Leonard is a worthy cause.
If there is to be one worthy cause.
let the cause be for this man
to walk free and take his place
beside ones who are wise.
Injustices visit each and
every hair above their high
cheekbones and earthy skin tone.
Leonard, Leonard. He walks
back and forth,
forth and back...

# A Man Who Drank Tea and Told Tales

Was he our Peter who stood
on the rock and laid the first
block to build
in his vision?
Just a man.
Kmtin, like Kmtin the mountain,
whose white assures us, calms us
with knowledge gained gazing
through silvery vapours
from intellectual heights.
Was he the air that surrounds us,
feeds us and eases us through
our journeys?
Our time continues
while his was then and is gone.
A man who saw beyond
to a time when his visions
would be fulfilled and forever
treasured by those who
called him a true Native Son,
Chapel Island's best.
A man who drank tea and told tales,
true meanings grasped
after the tea became cold.

## We Fight His Demons

As he gets older he becomes
more child-like.
Simple tasks, like bathing,
eating, dressing are now
hurdles he cannot, will not,
face alone.
Our hands are his tools
to use as required,
our roles reversed.
The child becomes
the doting parent.
Worries, doubts, fear
and finally acceptance.
We fight his demons.
We chase away the bad spirits,
and smooth away the
wrinkles of discord
within the circle.
The Mi'kmaq in him
knows the elders
will be cared for and it
begins with those
closest,
his own.

# Over Half a Century Ago

My days are slower now.
In my teens I was fast
like a corvette.
My days are a foggy blur,
as foggy as the Atlantic
over half a century ago.

Mud slows my walk.
As a child I loved it,
as a man in a trench,
I despised it.
Panzer tracks framed in
mud, heart racing.
A memory, just a memory
over half a century ago.

A tarmac with spilled fuel
filling my senses, roar of
spitfires sounding like
thunder at the farm
back home
over half a century ago.

Warriors of the sea,
land and sky, my
brothers and sisters.
We answered the call
over half a century ago.

## Mi'kmaw Maidens in Distress

Two young women with differences
as great as their height and colour.
The pair, troubles the same. For now
sharing my castle, shielded from
verbal slings and arrows.
Attacks causing great harm, esteem
damage and identity crisis.
Mi'kmaw maidens in distress like
sheep separated from the flock.
Wolves catching scent, circling.
Funny how the ones professing the
most love can profess such hate
for ones of their own blood.
Four walls getting smaller each
praising-
counselling-
cajoling-filled
day with the visiting
Mi'kmaw maidens in distress.
Armour becoming lacklustre,
as is my enthusiasm.

## Beyond Touch

I didn't want to tell you
how good you looked that day.
I wonder if it was the way our
sun attacked your eyes
and saw through a lash or two,
a man who sees you at night
although always beyond touch,
taste and smell.
Lay, lie, lying at night
overhead paint changing,
reflecting our moon.
My space. You stood so close
for a moment I knew you
inhaled our air a molecule
at a time.
How I saw the pride in the
manner of the voice and a
minute swelling of a breast.
It was your dusty white
digits gripping chalk from
our learning-together past.
Now back on soil and water
I must stand and fight
an urge to whisper the words
of a convincing wordsmith
to end our sporadic friendship,
becoming lovers of our time.

## For David

Sleep my son, sleep.
Dream of things fantastic
where new snow as
white as a winter cloud
lies like a soothing blanket.
Travel to far-off places,
remain safe and remember
I am never far from your side.
Do all the things young boys
do in their sleep. Touch the
stars, walk the moon, swim
the oceans without a care.
Visit the great thinkers of
time, imagine a language
of your own, teach the ones
you've met and never fear
saying the wrong thing.
Stretch your slumber wings
and fly to the home of the Eagle.
Ask him how he became
so important to the Mi'kmaq.
Tell him about the times
you saw him soar beneath the
clouds and how his shape
was silhouetted against white.
Remind him to come back for
the gatherings and let the
drums lull him to fly lazy
circles above our home.
Sleep my son, sleep.
And tomorrow when the sun
rises, I'll ask you about
your journey.

## Your Eyes

Your eyes cannot hide
the message of your
soul. Your manner is
not different, just your
eyes. Things happened
that made your eyes
lose their shine. Now
black pinpoints stare
down on me, making me
uncomfortable. A fly left
open? Something on
my face? I know we will
act differently now. Time
may change your soul and
eyes. Time may soften my
feelings. But for now, space you
shall have from me. Nothing
else.

## They Took Your Word

They took your word. How they
twisted, shaped and changed
your truth to their truth.
So easy for the sea of blues
to deceive the willing deceivable.
Intolerant truth seekers
who took away your rights.
Your brown eyes, hair and skin
no match against prejudicial
badges, crimson gowns and rubber gavels.
For four thousand days you knew.
We knew.
And they knew.
Two people, just two, without
fail strode beyond those walls
with stainless razor wire and
self-locking doors. Every month.
The great man, you his son,
we his people.
Each time, each visit
we were there in spirit.
The woman at his side.
a mother to you.
You felt the comfort,
heard the beat of her heart.
"Freedom!" robed ones said. Freedom
with strings attached.
"Admit to our truth. Admit to our
truth. For you, freedom.
For us, exorcism of guilt."
"No," you said
in your soft speaking voice.
"My word. My truth. My God."

So help you God.
You stayed in your cot and
awaited the arrival of your truth,
until a rust bucket galley cook,
impersonator of a master,
sharpened too many knives and
his forked pickled tongue
spat out your truth.
On that last day inside
the man and woman took
your unshackled hands
and led you through those
gates of hell,
to Freedom.

Those in green, not blue,
say the eels are not yours and
you cannot do as you wish.
These swimming broken pieces of
gallows rope, theirs not yours.
Badges, crimson gowns and rubber gavels
say so again.
Can the Creator sign contracts?
Did something happen
while we slept?
Now we wait.
We wait
and you wait again
for truth.

## My German Friend

My German friend, for ten years
you have been my neighbour and
now you speak to me for the
very first time.
In those ten years you have been
like a sponge, soaked and bathed
by friendly eager hands,
softly caressing you with dirty lies,
misconceptions and soapy versions
of history. My history. Our history.
Once again someone from across
has judged the cover and
failed to look inside.
The classic mistake.
For ten years you have lived in a bubble,
created by the biases of your friends.
And, yes, I believe you when you say,
"I'm not prejudiced." That kind of
prejudice is not of your making,
but it is made with your cooperation,
acceptance and willingness to
take someone else's ugliness and
call it your own.
You are horrified when I reveal the truth.
Fortunately I have a solution.
Come. Come see my home and sit at my table.
Let's go and see the people who work
as hard as you and your friends.
I'll take you to the source so an opinion
can be made using the
proper information and not other people's
borrowed eyes and hands and feet.

As a man who creates with wood, you must
understand that in order to make, to create,
you need the proper tools.
Here, I give you the tools. Now
you can use these implements to shape
an opinion of me, my people and our ways.
When you have learned all you can
you'll no longer have to rely on others
for your opinion. You'll have one of
your own.
Na to'q.

## For J. E. M.

A sunset passes silently
as one more day's designs
are met and silenced.
Your whispering breath
colours the still night.
Your love of yarns
paints your dreams.
Hands held subliminally
close to a dispensing heart,
known so well by me.
Inseparable like a thorn
and a rose.
Eyes of a summer sky
and mine of earth,
so much left to uncover.
Standing as one we see
our labour blossom
into the best of me
and the best of you.
Together we'll watch
till we become part
of the landscape.

Raindrops slide freely across
my darkened face.
Clan brothers lie still, waiting
for my song of death,
ready deep inside my throat.

*I Scream the Cry*

# I Scream the Cry

Raindrops slide freely across
my darkened face.
Clan brothers lie still waiting
for my song of death,
ready, deep inside my throat.
Silhouettes frozen,
the tools of death at rest for now,
charcoaled forest floor littered
with pine needles sticking to
leather and skin.
The enemy sleeps, all but one
tending fires, slowly
smoking meat for travel.
Forays into other sleeping camps
like ours, innocents
taken as they sleep.
Water fails to quench my need
for vengeance.
My knife feels heavy
as I scream the cry.

## No Match for Steel

A loam-filled spade
covers the poxed constant face,
the high cheekbones,
until dust.
A bow with broken sinew
laid quiet, no match for steel,
alongside a quiver half
empty.
Drum beating slower for the dead.
whispering feet, light of night,
death rattles, all joining
a chorus.
Birch bark canoes with pitch
cracking under a sun
aided by a wind heavy
with sorrow.
An empty lodge of mud, sticks,
and water, ripped open by a
surgeon, turned butcher.
Flattened grass springing to life,
moccasined feet caressing
seasoned paths strewn with barren
pots of clay.
Scent of sweetgrass gliding out,
fields almost bare now
receding toward
the sea.
Songs lie forgotten on sand, gentle
breezes scatter unspoken
lyrics, unplayed melodies.
A quiet moment.
A scream of life echoes within
a new wi'kuom, bouncing off the faces
of skin and granite, dispersing to a
forest reborn.

In 1996 the poem "No Match for Steel" was the winner of the Anne Marie Campbell Award for Creative Writing, an award given annually by the University College of Cape Breton to promising Cape Breton writers.

In choosing "No Match for Steel" the judge for the competition, Beatrice MacNeil, explained her choice as follows:

It pierces an arrow into the heart of yesterday and mourns the loss of a way of life so eloquently that one can hear the "whispering feet" and the "wind heavy with sorrow."

This writing is clear and haunting. It clears its throat of steel and screams for the scent of Sweetgrass to sweeten yesterday's lyrics. But the poet never loses completely. He is the moderator between time was and time is. His voice is the seed growing in the new forest. And the wind drifting softly by will wait and carry his words forever.

## Welamsitew

A pool of mountain-clear water
captures trees with gnarled
branches somewhat like an old
one with many winters. The sky lies quiet,
clouds and blue,
trapped in the little pool.
An insect dances, six legs causing
tiny ripples dying off before
reaching shore at the face of
Welamsitew, the vain one, who
sits and gazes at her mirrored self.
Cheekbones as high as the tops of
maples, last year's garments
lying, carpet-like, the colour of
sweat lodge flames bathing rocks.
A brown squirrel chats without
pause, disturbing no one except
Welamsitew, the vain one, and
causes her to lose her
loving gaze.
Viewing again, she closes her
eyes and opens them a
butterfly's wing depth at a time,
slowly and carefully until brown
eyes see a brown face, an
old friend, familiar lover,
herself.
The world of Welamsitew returns
to normal, clouds move on,
the sky begins to darken, waves
wash ashore erasing the walking
portrait of Welamsitew,
the vain one.

# For Ball and Shot

The winter rain never stops,
my feet are cold and I keep
longing for the warmth of
wi'kuom and my fire.
How I feel for the beaver,
his home at the tail of
this familiar lake.
Soon I will break open
his lodge of mud and stick
taking his young, his mate,
so that I may trade his life
and the lives of his clan
for ball and shot.
The bow pales beside the
musket balls and shot.
Once, a hunt would be silent,
with dignity, with acceptance,
now with great noise and
ceremony as a blazing tongue
bellows smoke and fire.
The cold wind swarms
over my clothed form.
Furs are gone,
traded for drink,
for ball and shot.
Lungs use less and less
of the morning air,
phlegm loosened
as I spray the slushy
grey snow, colouring it
like a summer sunset,
and then I hear a tail
slapping the once
familiar winter lake.

## Mainkewin?
## (Are You Going to Maine?)

Do you remember Maine?

Do you remember telling everyone who would listen that you
  were going to Vacation Land picking blueberries?

Do you remember the taste of your first submarine washed
  down with a cool Bud from the first store you saw after you
  crossed the border?

Do you remember the cool mornings that enabled you to get
  fifty plus boxes that first day at work there in the barrens?

Do you remember where you went swimming to cool off in
  afternoons? Was it Scoodic Lake or Columbia Falls?

Do you remember going back to the camp after picking blue-
  berries and seeing the filth on your body?

Do you remember waking up the next day and being unable
  to move without pain?

Do you remember working in the hot August sun not worry-
  ing about the UV index?

Do you remember being up half the night treating your badly
  burned red back and asking yourself, "What am I doing
  here?"

Do you remember the excitement of getting your first pay
  and spending it in Cherryfield, Millbridge or Ellsworth?

Do you remember the Bay Rum Pirates, Canned Heat Gang
  behind Grant's General Store?

Do you remember staying until the frost killed the best ber-
ries of the season, the ones that were
promised to you by the leaseholder?

Do you remember hurrying to get home so the kids could go
to school?

Do you remember the trip home and someone asking at the
border, "All Indians?"

## Shadows Dancing on the Edge

Photographs to petroglyph images,
beaded bone belts to fleeting
glimpses on sand swept clean
by wind and waves from distant
shores across the water of salt.
Stories so old, told around fire
pits as ancient as time.
Easy smiles seen in the dark
with shadows dancing on the
edge of the circle of light.
Knees pressed tightly to the
chest decorated with shells
white as the first snow, amulets
warding off spirits unkind to
the people who walk the woods.
Grandmother moon lends
her brilliance, illuminating the
questions that arise like mist in
the fields of sweetgrass near the shore.
When the morning sun touches
the tallest blade of swi-tey,
its mystic scent is dispersed
to far off places by the gentlest breeze,
No answers, just sensations
felt by those who are one
with their world.

# Ash and Flint Flying as One

Sinew stretches and bends
an unwilling sculpted
rock maple no longer
haughty in height and form.
A sinew loop encircles a ring
cut deep into the white
nakedness of aged wood.
An instrument of life and
death begins to take shape.
Flint on ash slides gently where
hand and bow meet like lovers.
A sound unique to sinew, ash
and maple is heard by the
holder, gripping as if his
very existence depends
upon a true flight.
The sound of fat burning,
odours rise like ghosts,
easily melding with smoke
and flame, revealing faces of
children crushing bones,
ripping meat and swallowing
between smiles, as the
provider of the cause of
celebration envisions
days of ash and flint
flying as
one.

Dear successive fathers:
Explain to me, please, when did the
change take place from owners
to wards of the selfish state?
Write down the reasons why
the land under our feet became
foreign soil in perpetuity...

*Clay Pots and Bones*

## Clay Pots and Bones

Dear successive fathers:
Explain to me please, when did the
change take place, from owners
to wards of the selfish state?
Write down the reasons why
the land under our feet became
foreign soil in perpetuity.
Say again how the signers of
1752 lost as much as they
gained while the ink from a
quill pen rested in its
blackened Royal well.
What justification exists that
allowed our mounds to be
desecrated, clay pots and bones.
Rock glyphs painted over by
cfc-propelled paint.
Our songs and stories protected
by copyright and law, not in the
bosom of our grandmothers or
grandfathers of yesterday.
The cost of keeping us does
not reflect the real cost.
How many ghostly sails with
reeking holds did English
ports comfort in early fog?
Have you much experience in
the destruction of people.
besides us?

# Dancing, Fasting and Praying

The Medicine Man
gazes intently like the Eagle,
as each of his charges
looks to him for answers.
The dancing, fasting and
praying are all in vain.
Each morning
the stronger ones
prepare the still ones
whose eyes and
features are frozen.
The summer village's vitality,
so strong for many seasons,
is now spent as if it
were a salmon.
Strangers, as pale as
ghosts, bear
gifts of trade,
leave with fur
and knowledge,
their hidden gift
to come later.
Brown faces,
red spots
spreading like a
summer fire,
consuming small ones
and old ones first.
The future, the past,
given the honours of
passing.
The Medicine Man
gazes intently,
as his eyes
water for the
last time.

# Kluskap and Mi'kmaw

*Kluskap:*
Who are you and what are you doing here?
Do you hear the forest?
It says, "Come to me and sit."

*Mi'kmaw:*
I sit here but I cannot hear.
I have forgotten.
I hear the one with shining eyes,
he tells me, "Run to me."

*Kluskap:*
Do not listen to him, listen to me.
He wants you for the wrong reasons.
He will steal your tongue, your land,
even where your ancestors are laid.

*Mi'kmaw:*
He does not want much,
a beaver, two fish, three geese.
When he gets these, he will be
satisfied and leave us.

*Kluskap:*
Listen carefully. The beaver will hide
from every man. Fish will be no more.
The goose will not come back. The land
he will take from you. And you cannot
say a word for he will have taken your
tongue. He will be here forever.

## Kluskap Aqq L'Nu

*Kluskap:*
Wen ki'l aq talueken tett?
Nutmn nipukt?
Teluek, "Juku'e
Aqq pa'si."

*L'Nu:*
Epi, pasik mu nutmu
Koqoey. Awan'ta'si'
Nutaq Wasoqwalkikwate'w,
Telimit, "Juku-tukwi'e'n."

*Kluskap:*
Mukk jiksituaw, jiksitui ni'n.
Ketanisk na pasik, kmutnattew na
kilnu, kmaqmikem aqq ma'w ko'kmaq
Ta'n elisulti'tij.

*L'Nu:*
Mu menuekekw pikwelk, pasik kopitl
Aqq tapusiliji mime'jk
Ne'siliji sinumkwaq,
Elmiaq ula msnaj, l'mietew.

*Kluskap:*
Nike' nute'n! Kaqietaqq kopitk,
Kaqietaqq mime'jk, sinumk ma' apja'sikw,
Apkwilja'tultew kmaqmikem,
Je ma'kis-taluewn mita kilnu ma'tenukw
Ma'liekw tami, siaw-i'tew na iapjiw.

## Leather, Stone and Bone

The cord has been with us
for such a long, long time.
Connected to the smiling
father, it grows taut from
our resistance and then
slackens again from
our reluctance.
The two sides:
flee, cut and be messy,
or stay, trust and be tidy.
One voice echoes the words
of ones who know,
their journeys complete,
the other voice of ones
who stay and breathe
the undated atmosphere.
Words written on parchment,
actors whose costumes
change with new acts
following written cues
making cultural-specific
laws governing the ones
of leather, stone and bone.
Cradle to grave, they say
Cradle to grave.
How words uttered in House
ring true to the present.
The giving father
smiles on.
The giving father
smiles on,
his children divided.
Cut or keep the cord.
No one asks the question.

## Save the Last Bullet

The noble savage – have we
dispelled the myth?
The monosyllabic dialogue
of unionized Mediterraneans
riding against The Duke
who passes out the guns,
telling the fair maiden,
"Save the last bullet
for yourself, in case..."
The great General who said,
"The only good Indian
is a dead Indian!"
as hundreds succumbed
behind his horse.
The General's horse stepped lighter,
the red dust became an
eternal dusty shroud.
Shed a tear with the children
of the Black Hills.
Sacred stone cut to provide
monumental caricatures
of men. All four.
*Consent forms required*
*to pray at the Hills!*
Is there a homeland
called Caucasia?

# The Chain Remains Strong

The Chain stretches back
four centuries.
Two different world views
met as equals.
A time when the numbers
were reversed.
Around a fire held by rock
they agreed.
For as long as the sun rises
and the rivers run.
Sacred oaths sworn.
Royal Proclaimer said his peace,
we ours.
Prosperity for all,
a new beginning.
Painted faces washed away
by the rain.
Wigs, leggings and blood
red coats rested.
The Chain remained strong,
held by men.
The land became deeded,
the game depleted.
Sister and brother beings
lost forever.
Equitable foes no longer,
a paradigm shift.
Hatchets at the ready,
knives honed.
Moose skin shields, no match
for disease.
The Chain remained strong,
revered by one.
Blankets of pox and vermin
a gift.

Sought-after hair still attached,
twenty pounds.
Survivors scattered but able
to stand.
The land became deeded,
the game depleted.
Dark robes singing psalms,
plundering others.
Lodges of learning where
no one spoke.
Tongues severed by words
and leather.
The Chain remains strong,
unforgotten.
Alive.

## Good Creator

Good Creator,
I bring sad news.
Let me sit closer to
the fire to warm
my aching bones.
Where shall I begin?
As you instructed us,
we fulfilled our bargain.
These woods, hills
and mountains echoed
the sounds of many
villages.
The animals you sent
were plenty
and we treated them
with respect.
We took no more
than we needed,
until...

Good Creator,
all this changed upon
the arrival of the ghost maker,
the pale one.
With his help, our
numbers shrivelled and died.
Now you must walk for days
to see other brown faces,
and they are but pale shadows
of the ones who have gone
forever.

Good Creator,
our robes are in tatters,
our stomachs like empty
seashells. Sand
and dust.

Good Creator,
my hands are the hands
of a disrespectful child
who has taken too much.
The woods are empty now,
devoid of sound,
like a sunset or a passing cloud.

Good Creator,
I seek your counsel.
Is it too late?

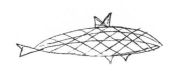

For you I say keep your skin
the colour of earth and your
grandchildren like eagle wings.
Teach the ear so it hears
your young speak our words.

*Now It's Your Turn*

## Now It's Your Turn

Look. Just look at it now
My grandfather's grandfather could
walk for two days before seeing
the ones with wanting eyes.
Now today I can't walk more
than fifteen minutes and I am
reminded by a sign that this
land is no longer ours to do
with as we see fit.
I yearn for those days when
I caught all the fish I could eat,
the rest shared with others.
My canoe would be filled to
the gunwales, her ribs bulging
as she strained to take me
home with salmon.
The trees offer little shade now.
Do you know why?
They have been cut so much
they don't get a chance
to grow. When I was young
I saw a tree so big
ten men could stand on it.
Grandson, listen to me.
Make me a promise that you will
not let us lose any more.
The land that is gone stays gone.
The fish will be wary and may
never come back.
The trees may grow back,
if left alone.

For you I say keep your skin
the colour of earth and your
grandchildren like eagle's wings.
Teach the ear so it hears
your young speak our words.
My eyes have seen many things,
now it's your turn.
Taho.

# Questions for Great Grandfather

Have you ever felt the kiss
of a tanned hide cured by
your hands?
Do you remember how
balsam wood smelled after
a summer rain?
Tell me how supple birch
bark becomes while wet
outside your canoe.
Has your hand fought with
a salmon at the end of your
bone-tipped spear?
When was the last time you
sat with bare back against
a bleached stump?
How many times have you
shaped your hair with black
bear grease?
How long did you lie on the
green grass, belly down, before
the sun reminded you?
What happened to your bare
feet when you walked across
a boggy swamp?
Has your tongue ever tasted the
ocean from an oyster eaten
fresh from the shore?
Were you able to tell which bird
sang the loudest on the morning
of the solstice?
When you lay down under the stars
did you find where Great Bear
hid from Chickadee?

Great Grandfather, I have seen things,
faces that turned scarlet when struck
with venomous words.
I heard the sound of glass falling
onto an unkempt green blanket.
Ask me about the sound of bone
breaking again,
the sound of a door slamming, locked,
not meant for elements.
Spoken words meaning less, foreign
with each syllable.
Stolen childhoods, crushed ideas,
frozen gazes.
Great Grandfather, I have also heard
words whispered at dawn,
seen the flash of fire in the
eyes of those who survive.
Stood with those rich with
pockets bare as their feet.
Heard the drum beat louder,
so loud it shakes the inside.
Songs of times gone by
in the mouths of the young.
Great Grandfather, from a
cupped hand over battered
chest,
I release you.

## Matuesuey Kmtin
## (Porcupine Mountain)

A plume of grey rises from the
heights of Matuesuey Kmtin.
A shudder felt, muffled sounds
escape as each new charge
catches current, releasing rock.
With each passing day Kmtin
dwindles, a fading shadow,
yet still dwarfing bulk carriers that
come seeking cargo to cover
the green with slabs of grey
in cities south and west,
in lands intent on concealing
silent footpaths of those who roamed.
Across the man-made road
of rock, over the once fluid
now semi-stagnant bluish
green-grey highway
of whales and tuna,
a message is posted:
*Turn Off All Radios*
*Danger*
*Blasting Area.*
What if I left my radio on?
Would they leave Matuesuey
Kmtin alone?
The owners of this shrinking hill
will leave only when Matuesuey
Kmtin is a memory found in
obscure poems by an obscure
poet who lacked the resolve to
play his radio and sing along
momentarily preventing its
determined demise.

# Learned Elder

Learned Elder, share with me
the universal truths that you
harbour deep within your soul.
Take me by the hand to that
special place.
Lead the way so that I may
see the prints on Mother Earth.
Give me guidance, teach me
to ask and not to demand.
Sing to me the chants of old so I
may keep them alive.
Take out your drum and let the
sound reverberate inside.
Show the steps of the sacred fire,
offer tobacco and sweetgrass.
Unclench your hand and soak the
birch bark and shape a wi'kuom.
Hone your knife and scrape the fat
from the fresh hide of the kopit.
Use your ancient axe and bring
down the straight and true ash.
Weave your baskets to hold the
summer bounty of berries.
Polish that special rock to
make your dream stone.
Share the stories of my clan,
give me my history for safe keeping
until the time comes when I
become the Learned Elder.

## Fires of the Ancients

Stand together as one.
Speak together as one.
Use all fifty-two languages
in this land of the maple.
How can they not hear us
when we speak so powerfully
revealing ugliness so beautifully?
Wise words of ancestors.
A voice alone is like a
solitary morning dew drop.
Voices together become rivers
of dreams, destinies and aspirations.
Let's do what we say.
Let's say what we do.
Speak the words spoken around
fires of the ancients.
A single shout becomes a
chorus that no one
dare drown.

## Our Nation World

My eyes are wet
with the tears
of our loss.
As I stand alone
on the shore, on
top of these blue
rocks, I think back
to a time when all
voices heard were
in our language.
The very same that
Kluskap used to
teach the Mi'kmaq
about the ways of
our Nation World.
Now as I stand here,
the salt spray
washes away any
trace of my sadness.
I know now that
I will hear those
voices again as
I hear now the voices
of the Spirits who
speak to me through
Mother Earth.

The ready drum sounds like a crack
of thunder as you move as fast as light
around a sacred fire, with the smell of
sweetgrass and sage trailing
behind you like wisps of mist.
Dancer, you bring joy to the soul.

*Magic Steps*

## Magic Steps

Dancer, you bring joy to the soul.
How you move as quiet as a cloud
casting shadows above it all,
hair the colour of a raven's wing,
leather and beads absorbing light,
dancing back in time when your
magical steps would be your mother's.
The silent drum held over a fire,
stretching, becoming taut while
you, dancer, recount the steps
your mother would have danced to.
The ready drum sounds like a crack
of thunder as you move as fast as light
around a sacred fire, with the smell of
sweetgrass and sage trailing
behind you like wisps of mist.
Dancer, you bring joy to the soul.
How you move across time, taking
me back to a time when your
steps would be your mother's.
The drum held by your father,
holding it over a fire, the same
way his father would have done,
stretching, making it taut,
waiting for the swish of
moccasin as it touches grass
made flat by others who dance
the magic steps of old.

# A Ball of Blue

The elders stand quiet,
no words, just their presence
charging the misty morn.
Mi'kmaw drummers, their
leather-bound sticks
at the ready, tap a gentle
beat against leather,
bead and feather.
Flags fly with the slightest
of breezes caressing the faces
of the frozen dancers.
The sacred fire accepts
tokens of sage,
sweetgrass and gold-like tobacco.
Offerings and silent prayers
tossed into a fire which
lives for such favours.
The distant relations,
heads lowered, wait for a signal.
Then, at once the drum speaks,
snapping everyone back to the
present in time and in space.
The circle comes alive with
music and the fluidity of dance.
Smiles seen as broad as the mist-free
horizon with blues and whites
of sparse clouds dancing their
eternal dance around a ball of blue
we call home.

## On the Shore of Bras d'Or

A storm with thunder and lightning,
an anomaly on a December day,
destroys a Chapel that stood alone
on the shore of Bras d'Or.

Wooden pegs in place of nails,
house of God framed by hand on
an isle sacred to the People of the Dawn
on the shore of Bras d'Or.

Touching sky as high as any
on Cape Breton Isle, a steeple that
cast a shadow in all directions
on the shore of Bras d'Or.

Until a flash of fire ignited the cross,
yellow and orange flames danced
the day while an inferno roared
on the shore of Bras d'Or.

With waves as high as a man
breaking foam and fury over
the lone boat, unable to help
on the shore of Bras d'Or.

Awestruck congregation, faces
wet from tears and elements,
witnessing an act of God
on the shore of Bras d'Or.

As each piece of timber trembled
and fell, a cry in unison heard
over the blare of the storm
on the shore of Bras d'Or.

Chains of light last seen in
the heat of summer returned
in the cold of winter to lay waste
on the shore of Bras d'Or.

Time came when ashes cooled,
soot and spark were raised by wind,
and fire an all-too-recent memory,
on the shore of Bras d'Or.

A bell forged from a distant
foundry, large, heavy and loud,
was nowhere to be found
on the shore of Bras d'Or.

Some said an accident caused
by lack of foresight. Others said
a warning from our Grandmother who lives
on the shore of Bras d'Or.

## Grey Skies, White Mist

Riding waves in an open boat of
blue on a morning with steady
rain coming down on an American
Day of Independence.
No parades today.
The wind blowing gently upon the
red faces of my brothers, one younger,
the other older.
Indulging in a common quest,
salmon.
Taking the time to make memories.
Grey skies, white mist,
net empty as our stomachs.
Maybe tomorrow, knives sharpened.
The trip back in drizzle,
washing faces, minds and
souls.

# Progress

Handshakes, smiles all around. The
suits come into the band office
carrying their pens.
Fast polite chatter, wet palms
hiding papers piled like a pyre
inside leather boxes with brass locks.
Minions of the queen mentioning her
thorny hat, this and that and the Act.
Words spoken with no "ahs" or "ays."
The counselled Council listens
to the Concord pitch, its pros and cons,
weighing each grain against each rock.
Four plaque-like walls holding their eyes,
seeing nothing new or different
since the last time.
Mouthpiece spinning spiels,
nods of non-comprehension,
feathers combed not ruffled,
patted not struck.
Sign here, initial there, witness here.
More handshakes,
dry palms wet again.
Saunter out of the old Indian Day School,
now band office, boxes go out with white
blisterless hands,
clutching pens like Cornwallis trophies.
Black ink slowly drying with red splatters
here, there...

# From Wind and Prying Eyes

Almost hidden by a colluding maple
one hundred yards away, a man
with dun coloured hair moving
rhythmically to a primeval metre,
keeping time with another
unseen by eyes but his own.
A red skeleton of unknown
genus is being covered by the
workers continuing their role
as inattentive voyeurs.
Wind picks up, leaves begin to
shudder, their milky undersides
exposed to the harsh
judging tight. Wind foregoes
interest, calming, slowing.
Leaves green again, their verdant
veins once more concealed
from wind and prying eyes.

# Shadow Dancers at Night

My shadow dances as I move
toward the rising sun.
I am not a dancer but my shadow
dances smoothly and with purpose.
When I pause,
the dancing stops,
the music of the drum
silent.
As I go faster,
tempo picks up,
cadence matches sounds
heard only by my shadow.
The dancer hides, sacred steps
seen only from the corner of the eye.
Forgotten dancer hides from
the noonday sun until time
comes to remind,
go back.
My shadow dances as I move
toward the setting sun.
Dancing smoothly and with purpose,
growing ever larger, impatient,
needing to break free,
till the sun hides from night
and my shadow disappears,
joining shadow dancers
at night.

## One More Night

The old man sat crouched beside a fire
feeling each bone in his ancient frame
cry in protest as he circled a small
area to lay his aged form to rest.
Not unlike brother Paqtism the wolf
who would search the four directions and
give each a cursory sniff ensuring that he
not be surprised by visitors of night.
The old man cupped his brown hands, scored
from his struggles of eighty summers,
and began to speak in a voice of one who
knows and has travelled the good path.
Lu'ks, I am at rest and the fire burns
brightly permitting me to see your
eyes and know that you understand, for
what I am about to tell you I have kept
close to my heart for sixty summers.
Now pay close attention and remember
you must not tell anyone this story until
I have moved on to a place not here under
these stars. See how chickadee tries to
catch the great bear? Ah, the bear will
hide but the chickadee will be persistent and
cook the bear in his pot. See how the pot
points? The pot is never far from the bear.
That is why the bear can never hide and he
loses his life each year and starts all over
again. Believe me, I have seen them do the
same dance the last seventy summers.
Forgive me, my body stays but my mind
wanders to places not yet discovered by us,
the Mi'kmaq, the Children of the Dawn.
Uncle, are you sleeping?

No! Just resting my eyes.
What about the story you have kept for
sixty summers, will you share it?
Oh that. No, not tonight, maybe tomorrow
night. It has been with me for sixty summers,
one more night isn't going to hurt.

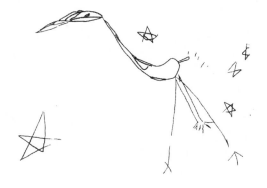

# My Paddle Does Not Sing

My paddle does not sing
when I dip it into the clear
summer waters of Indian Lake.
This wood of ash, shaped
by a distant knife, cuts cleanly
and with each stroke creates
miniature vortexes drawing
me away from the sounds of
the shore and sky, back to
times of birch bark and pitch.
Even the predictable thunder of
the Concord with its race
against sound does not deter
me from my journey back.
Back to times when the lake
would have echoed the sounds
of knives scraping hides on
the shore and of little ones
chasing each other among
alders and grass as tall as they.
The water reeds play a
symphony as they caress the
underside of my kwitn,
my transport to lilies.
Summer flies dance just above
the surface, tempting the hungry
ones from below the clear summer
waters of Indian Lake.
A transport truck rattles by,
bellowing air, ending my travel
back in time. The wind changes
as I guide my kwitn back to
shore, back to our time,
back to now.

# The Blackened Hole

A naked man runs out
of a burning house,
his screams silenced by
the acrid by-product
of toxins, varnished wood,
and petrochemicals.
The resourceful volunteers
strain to hear his last sounds
but only gasps and pained
noises escape his charred
mouth. He falls. No one
catches him. His chest
rises silently then stops
in mid-breath.
The fire continues to
engulf, casting an illuminated
shadow on the pitch dark
night. Stars blink as they
have always done. The
morning stops the night
in its tracks.
The blackened hole where
the house once stood holds
secrets soon to be covered
by the newly arrived
idling bulldozer,
standing at attention
like a pallbearer,
doubling as an anxious
grave digger who gets
paid by commission.

# The Church of the Council

The room was packed with faces,
young and old, from near and far,
all here for one purpose – to discuss
the state of affairs of the religion of
The Church of the Council which
was affiliated with The Thirteenth
House of Whoever Was in Power.
This was an annual event which drew
many to hear the words of the old
and wise ones who were elected to
their positions on The Church of
The Council. The Church was a
not-for-profit organization and seldom
ever in fiscal shape due to the
lack of fiscal restraint and exercise.

Now the white-haired ones
had a plan but in order for this plan
to pass and be implemented, it needed
the support of the dark-haired ones
who were the majority and unruly.
The Speaker rose from his great seat
and began to address the congregation
in a slow and deliberate manner.
The speech was long and between
naps the wisest of the wise heard the
words and was slowly lulled to his
usual spot in dreamland, which was
far more interesting than the speech
of the Speaker, entering its second
full hour. Then at the exact time when
the Speaker was to launch his third
hour, a sound was heard from the back of
the room. A dark-haired one stood. The room
fell quiet as he made his way to the
centre of the Great Hall and stopped amidst

the rows of white-haired ones to his right
and dark-haired ones to his left. All were
facing the Great Chair in which sat the
Speaker who was shocked into silence at
being so rudely interrupted. He sat with
his hands and mouth open in mid-sentence.

The dark-haired one said in a loud, clear
voice that everyone in the hall heard,
"I have sat here and listened to the Speaker
for two full hours and yet I have not
heard anything I have not heard before.
These points that he makes can be found
in the minutes from last year's assembly.
I suspect as usual the only person who has
read the minutes is the person who has copied
in quill our script. My question is this: why do
keep repeating the same things year after year?"
With this simple question the room exploded
with more questions similar in nature.

As quickly as they came, they went their separate
ways, never to meet again. The Church of the
Council was expelled from The Thirteenth House
of Whoever Was in Power.

Rain falling slowly on my
Red Native Canadian back.
Sensations evoke a soft
Touch of a woman I knew,
Once, only once.

*Once, Only Once*

## Once, Only Once

Rain falling slowly on my
Red Native Canadian back.
Sensation evokes the soft
touch of a woman I knew,
once, only once.
Warm caress of cloud water
spreading throughout.
A lonely large drop sliding
down my shoulder past
the curve of my back
Falling and hitting the deck.

## Idling

Sitting with idling thoughts,
intangible mind pollution.
Eyes like glass steaming up.
drawing fleeting images.
Fiery orb staring down
from its distant height,
changing everything to its
terms and conditions,
effecting and affecting
my outlook inside this
cranium capsule of time.

## Tasks and Demands

I walk into my cluttered space,
screen stares back, waiting
for tasks and demands.

A call comes in from a member
who is dissatisfied with her lot
and wants to spend an hour in
confessional, but I have no collar.
When we finish, she talks with
less strain while my shoulders
sag under her adopted burdens.
Someone knocks.

Screen flashes warnings as
flying windows dance across
the single cube-like glass eye.

Another soul starts with shouts,
anger pulsing through his veins.
Stories of leaking windows,
dripping taps and front end jobs
on a new car purchased with a
child-tax-credit downpayment. No
questions, just money and the first
month free from payment or guilt.
Potholes causing wear and tear.
"How can I get my cheque
when the roads are so bad?"
I answer, "We'll try harder next time."
He shouts, "My vote I'll keep,
you'll not get it this year."
"Suit yourself."

All alone now except for flying windows
patiently awaiting tasks and demands.

## Our Hearts Were Beating One With Their Drum

They were drumming for the one
we were mourning.
A walk with my son from
our talk, our sharing,
Our pain.
We saw the brightest
star. We knew who,
our burden less.
All alone except for our pain.
the blue-black night,
and the drum.
We both heard it, music for
two battered hearts walking as one.
It began to change us.
Our hearts were beating
one with their drum,
healing.
They were drumming for the one
we were mourning.
We heard them give their hearts
to the drum for their friend,
for our boy, cousin, Godson.
The days are better now,
moments of silence.
Our hearts were beating
one with their drum.
They were drumming for the one
we were mourning.

## Dreams Not Wanted

Who are you?
    Chief
    Poet
    Man
    Father
    Husband
    Son
    Brother
    Relation
    Friend
    Connection
similar to the silky strands of a spider's web
capturing light and sustenance, keeping out
dreams not wanted.

# A Work in Progress

Snowflakes, as white as
can be, fall easily,
melting upon contact
with the open palm of
my outstretched hand.
I raise it to the heavens
as an offering, a sacrifice
to the silent descending
pure grace.
The artist from afar
dispenses the solitary
colour as if to shroud
one of Vincent's starry nights.
My gauche hand feels lighter,
allowing it to rise higher
as the vapour from my breath
slowly ascends and drifts
aimlessly away from
my moment of tribute.
The severed reminder,
complaints of phantom pain,
nothing.
Flesh versus steel,
steel wins. Flesh loses
to the gods of tomorrow.
All arrangements complete,
the service at sunrise
for a nail, a bone, a scrap of flesh.
And the eulogy,
a work in progress.

## Dance Along the Ghost Highway
## (Translation)

The fire warms and comforts him.
fixing his gaze.
They call him
the Old One Who Knows,
the young men
whose hair is black as night.
while his a reminder of a winter
that is never far away.
The fire leaps,
throwing sparks
into the moonless night.
All is ready for stories,
the gift of past ones
who dance along the ghost highway.
They light the pipe,
and tobacco smoke
clouds each man's face
like the morning fog
as it rises from the lake.
He remembers as a boy
how he would sit
as quiet as a shadow
listening to the Old Ones
recount hunts, hungers and wars.
Now the stories are ready.
He knows those
who sit with him tonight
will remember.
He is slow to start,
slow to eat
and slow to move.
Finally, with the voice of thunder
he begins to weave a story

## Skite'kemrujewey Awti

Kisikuo'p elisink kikjuk puktewiktuk,
Puktew tele'k kutey mimajikek,
ke's puksuk pijekemk te's wnaqiaq,
kutey kloquejk alayjita'jik,
aqq mikwite'tk ta'n tuju
nutqwe'kek i'tla'tekes,
l'pa'tu'jijuijek nekm mikwite'tmajik
kisiku'k eloqisultijik kikjiw puktukewiktuk,
kikto'qipultijik, kikto'qamkipultijik,
aknutma'tijik.
Msit wen a'tukwet aqq kwetmtijik,
tmaweyey wtlu'tew alayja'sik
msit tami wsiskuk kutey
eksitpu'kewey u'n ke'sk kwetmaj,
jiksitmawet, jiksitk a'tukwaqn.
Ankite'tk, poqji mikwite'tkl a'tukwaqnn,
poqji ankite'tkl kisiku'k wtayjual,
ankite'tk a'tukwaqn ta'n tewije'k,
wen aqsutkis, wen mawtmk telues,
poqji ankite'tk ta'sisni'k kisiku'k
kikto'qi pemkopultijik puktewiktuk
aqq weskewo'ltijik.
Tal lukutisni'k etuk na'kwek,
waisisk al'kwilua'tijik,
al'kwilmu'tij ta'n i'taq aqq msit
tami elapa'sin oqnitpa'q
aqq kejia'tiji skite'kmujk eymu'tijik.
Na kisikuo'p apaja'sit,
alapa'sit puktewiktuk,
nutqo'ltite'wk ankama'titl
askise'nmi'tij puktew,
wel pmiaq puktew,
wenaqapa'sit, wasoqa'latl wtmaqnml,

from a fire pit
long forgotten.
Under these stars
that seem to dance
in rhythm with his voice,
the time is right.

illama'teket, na poqj aknutk,
poqji a'tukowajik nutqo'ltite'wk,
ankamajik aqq nemi'sit aqq kejitoq
nekm nike'ankamut,
nekm nike' jiksitut aqq nekm nike'kisiku.
kisiku ata'a'tukwet.

Two New Poems

# Demasduit

*In the National Library and Archives Preservation Centre*

I saw sights
no one from my tribe
has ever seen.
I saw paintings of canoes,
of birch bark wi'kuoms,
and brown faces
encased in oil.
In these crypts
where the temperature is perfect
the humidity constant,
paintings, sealed off
from man and catastrophe.

She was the last
known image of a race,
a tribe.

She was wrapped in a fur stole,
and her eyes looked out and saw
she was the last known image.

She was Mary March,
she is Demasduit.

As the drawer rolled shut
and she returned to the stony silence of her crypt,
awaiting the next generation,

I wept.

## Our Sisters

Our sisters –
Who has seen them last?
The 824 who speak
No more, nowhere,
Their songs fell silent,
Their trail on glassed ice
Rubbed away till gone.

Speak – we must speak
Dance – we must dance
Warn others – we must warn
Search – we must search

Our sisters
Our mothers
Our aunts
Our cousins
Our friends
Without you the pain grows
Without answers
More will be taken.

No more.

Taho.